PUMPKIN THE FARM DETECTIVE

THIS BOOK BELONGS TO

_____

FOR THE KIDS WHO WANT TO EXPLORE

ISBN: 9798894583099

ON FARMER JOE'S FARM, A BRIGHT ORANGE CAT NAMED PUMPKIN WATCHED OVER THE PUMPKIN PATCH EVERY NIGHT.

HE LOVED HIS PUMPKINS. BIG ONES, TINY ONES
AND THE ROUNDEST OF THEM ALL!

BUT ONE MORNING, PUMPKIN WOKE UP TO A SHOCKING SIGHT—ONE
OF THE BIGGEST PUMPKINS WAS GONE!

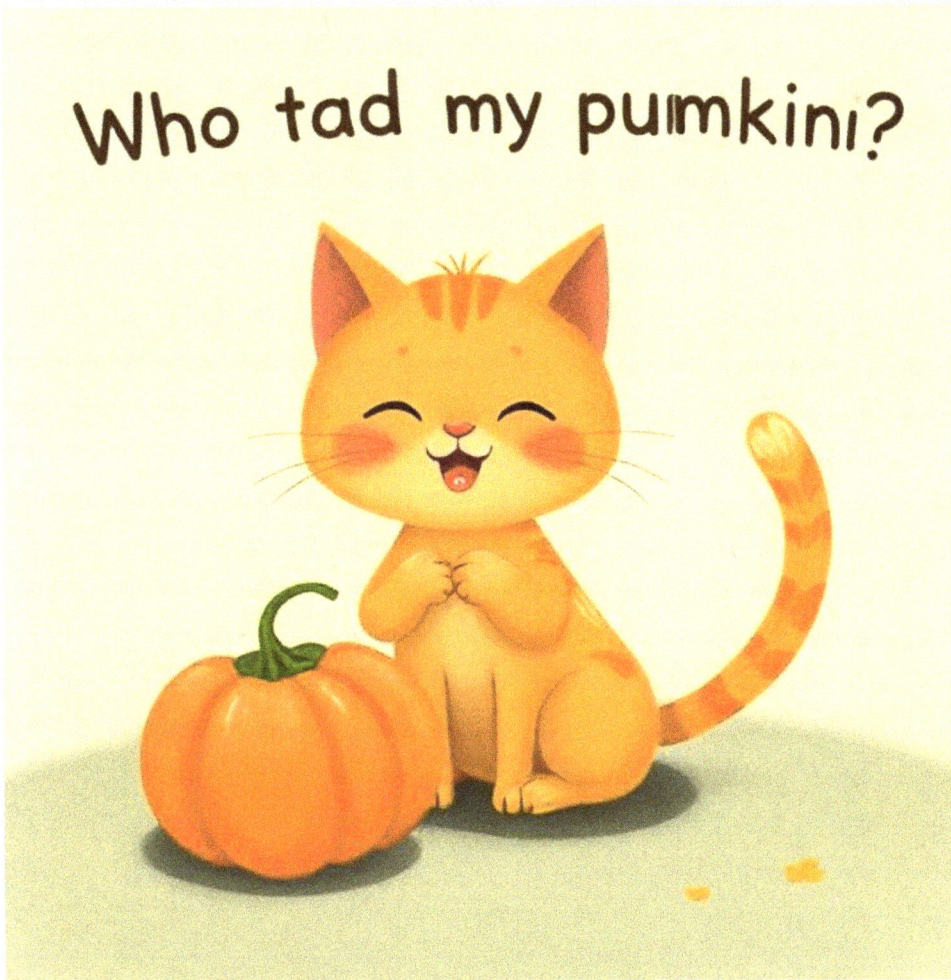

"WHO TOOK MY PUMPKIN?" PUMPKIN MEOWED, HIS TAIL TWITCHING.

HE SNIFFED THE GROUND. TINY PAW PRINTS LED AWAY FROM THE PATCH.

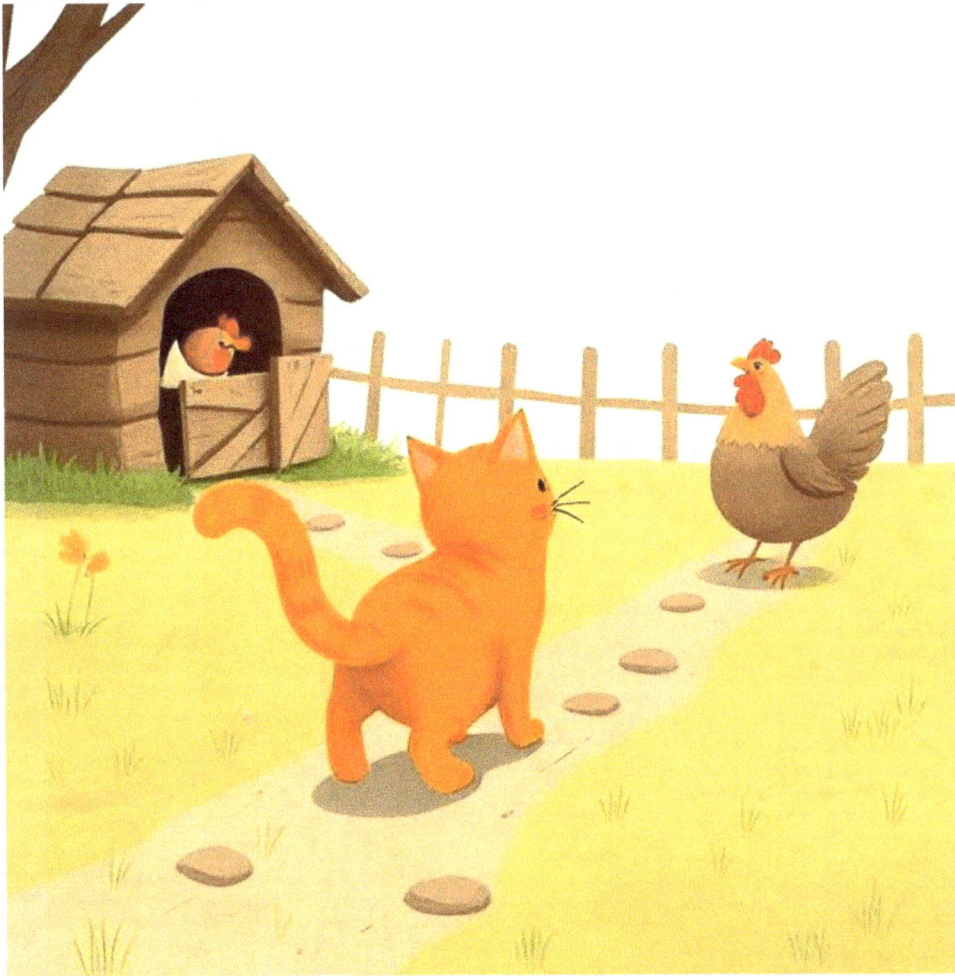

PUMPKIN FOLLOWED THE TRACKS PAST THE CHICKEN COOP, WHERE HENNY THE HEN CLUCKED.

Henny, did you see who clamy pumkhn?.

"HENNY, DID YOU SEE WHO TOOK MY PUMPKIN?" PUMPKIN ASKED.

"NOT ME !" HENNY SQUAWKED.
"I ONLY EAT CORN ! MAYBE CHECK NEAR THE HAYSTACK."

PUMPKIN PADDED TO THE HAYSTACK,
WHERE BENNY THE BUNNY WAS NIBBLING A CARROT.

"BENNY, DID YOU SEE MY MISSING PUMPKIN?" PUMPKIN ASKED BENNY.

"Nope!"

something
bin a earh!
bibonial it.

BENNY TWITCHED HIS NOSE, "NOPE! BUT I SAW SOMETHING ROLLING
TOWARD THE BARN LAST NIGHT!"

PUMPKIN'S EARS PERKED UP. HE HURRIED TO THE BARN.

INSIDE, THE COWS WERE DOZING AND THE BARN SMELLED OF FRESH HAY.

"DAISY, DID YOU SEE A ROLLING PUMPKIN?" PUMPKIN ASKED THE BIGGEST COW.

DAISY YAWNED. "I DID HEAR A THUMP IN THE NIGHT. MAYBE CHECK NEAR THE OLD OAK TREE."

PUMPKIN DASHED TO THE OAK TREE, WHERE THE WISE OLD OWL,
OLIVER, SAT ON A BRANCH.

Oliiveer, did a seee my uunpki??

"OLIVER, DID YOU SEE MY PUMPKIN?" PUMPKIN CALLED UP.

OLIVER BLINKED. "A PUMPKIN?
YES! IT ROLLED PAST HERE... CHASED BY SOMETHING SMALL AND FLUFFY!"

PUMPKIN'S FUR BRISTLED. "SMALL AND FLUFFY? WHO COULD THAT BE?"

HE CREPT BEHIND THE TREE AND GASPED—A TINY CHIPMUNK WAS
NIBBLING ON HIS PUMPKIN!

"HEY! THAT'S MY PUMPKIN!" PUMPKIN MEOWED.

THE CHIPMUNK FROZE, CHEEKS FULL OF PUMPKIN SEEDS.

"I... I DIDN'T MEAN TO STEAL IT!" THE CHIPMUNK SQUEAKED. "IT ROLLED AWAY, AND I GOT HUNGRY."

Rolled awey?

PUMPKIN TILTED HIS HEAD. "ROLLED AWAY?"

"YES!" THE CHIPMUNK POINTED. "IT WAS SO WINDY LAST NIGHT! THE PUMPKINS ROLLED ALL OVER THE PLACE!"

PUMPKIN'S WHISKERS TWITCHED. COULD THE WIND HAVE STOLEN HIS PUMPKINS?

HE LOOKED AROUND. MORE PUMPKINS WERE MISSING!

PUMPKIN CLIMBED THE OLD OAK TREE FOR A BETTER VIEW.

HE SAW A TRAIL OF PUMPKINS LEADING TOWARD THE RIVER!

"OH NO! THEY'RE FLOATING AWAY!" PUMPKIN GASPED.

HE RACED TO THE RIVERBANK AND SAW HIS PUMPKINS BOBBING IN THE WATER.

WITH A GREAT LEAP, PUMPKIN PADDLED INTO THE RIVER AND NUDGED THEM BACK TO SHORE.

THE CHIPMUNK AND BENNY THE BUNNY HELPED PUSH THE PUMPKINS
ONTO DRY LAND.

FARMER JOE ARRIVED. "PUMPKIN! YOU SOLVED THE MYSTERY!" HE SAID,
SCOOPING UP THE WET CAT.

PUMPKIN PURRED PROUDLY. "THE WIND WAS THE REAL PUMPKIN THIEF!"

Pumpkin!

FARMER JOE CHUCKLED. "YOU'RE THE BEST FARM DETECTIVE, PUMPKIN!"

THAT NIGHT, PUMPKIN CURLED UP IN THE PUMPKIN PATCH, GUARDING HIS ROUND, ORANGE FRIENDS.

AND FROM THEN ON, FARMER JOE BUILT A FENCE TO KEEP THE
PUMPKINS FROM ROLLING AWAY AGAIN!

PUMPKIN SMILED. NO MORE MISSING PUMPKINS—JUST A PEACEFUL FARM UNDER THE STARS.

AND IF THE WIND EVER TRIED AGAIN, PUMPKIN WOULD BE READY!

www.ingramcontent.com/pod-product-compliance
Lightning Source LLC
LaVergne TN
LVHW081702050326
832903LV00026B/1866